Young Pathfinder 2

Games and fun activities

*O*ther titles in the series

Grammar is fun (YPF8)
by Lydia Biriotti

This book combines games with meticulous attention to grammar and syntax in language teaching for young children. Learning languages through games can both be fun and develop grammatical awareness! Examples and activities are provided in French, but the ideas and methodology are applicable to other languages.

Making the link (YPF7)
by Daniel Tierney and Malcolm Hope

This book gives guidance on how to teach a foreign language to young learners by linking it to other areas of the curriculum. This approach has the advantage that the teacher may be able to reinforce in the foreign language, concepts already developed through other related curriculum work.

Let's join in! (YPF6)
by Cynthia Martin with Catherine Cheater

This book brings together a collection of rhymes, poems and songs which have proved motivating for learners from three to thirteen. It is intended as a practical resource for both specialist and non-specialist teachers of French and German at primary level and for teachers at Key Stage 3 who would like ideas to complement their coursebook. It also provides teachers of less frequently taught languages with ideas which they can adapt to their own needs.

First steps to reading and writing (YPF5)
by Christina Skarbek

This book investigates how much can be done at the early stages of foreign language teaching to prepare young learners for reading and writing. The aim is to ensure that young learners remain interested and motivated, to get them accustomed to working with written text and for them to enjoy experimenting with words.

Keep talking: teaching in the target language (YPF4)
by Peter Satchwell

This book builds on the initial experience of the primary teacher of introducing the foreign language into the classroom. It provides detailed guidance on how to ensure progression by developing the use of the language further, by encouraging pupil to teacher and pupil to pupil talk with a limited but well-planned range of the target language (examples from French and German).

Are you sitting comfortably? Telling stories to young language learners (YPF3)
by Daniel Tierney and Patricia Dobson

How to keep learners spellbound and develop their listening skills in the target language at the same time. The authors provide guidelines on the type of stories that work well in the foreign language. They look at different ways of presenting stories, preparation for storytelling and follow-up activities.

Catching them young (YPF1)
by Peter Satchwell and June de Silva

This book provides guidance on how to integrate foreign language teaching into the primary curriculum. It suggests ways of setting up and implementing a foreign language course, covering teaching aims and methodologies, resources and course content. It addresses the issue of learner progression from primary to secondary school and contains numerous ideas for classroom activities.

All CILT Publications are available from good book suppliers or directly from: **Grantham Book Services Ltd,** Isaac Newton Way, Alma Park Industrial Estate, Grantham, Lincs NG31 9SD. Tel: 01476 541 080. Fax: 01476 541 061.

Young Pathfinder 2

A CILT series for primary language teachers

Games and fun activities

Cynthia Martin

CiLT
Centre for Information
on Language Teaching and Research

The views expressed in this book are those of the author and do not necessarily represent the views of CILT.

First published 1995
Copyright © 1995 Centre for Information on Language Teaching and Research
ISBN 1 874016 41 0

Cover by Neil Alexander
Printed in Great Britain by Copyprint UK Ltd

Published by the Centre for Information on Language Teaching and Research,
20 Bedfordbury, Covent Garden, London WC2N 4LB.

Contents

Introduction

This Young Pathfinder focuses on ways of introducing and carrying out activities in the foreign language which are particularly suited to young learners below the age of eleven. However, many of the games could be used with learners in Years 7 and 8, or be enjoyed by children with special educational needs.

It aims to provide practical support for primary class teachers who may be relatively new to foreign language teaching and would welcome suggestions for activities to practise simple structures often introduced in the early stages of a foreign language programme. It also intends to encourage and inform teachers who are considering offering young pupils the experience of a foreign language, whether within the main school day, after school or in Saturday morning language clubs. Examples - mainly in French, with some in German - are given of some tried and tested ideas. However, all activities are adaptable for use in several languages.

As there is currently no statutory requirement to teach a foreign language before the age of eleven, the pattern of provision in UK primary schools varies widely. This Young Pathfinder does not offer a scheme of work or a course, but it does provide some ideas for practical activities which can be drawn upon whether you are teaching a foreign language as a discrete subject within the primary day, or whether you are embedding it in aspects of daily classroom life.

The suggestions offered are not the only approach and you are encouraged to select from the variety of strategies suggested to make the ideas 'your own'. For this reason, there is also a section on creating your own games and making materials.

As many primary teachers are not foreign language specialists, most of the games and activities have examples of suggested target language instructions to be used by the teacher when setting up the games. There are also some examples of game-playing language to enable pupils to play in small groups where appropriate.

What do we mean by a 'game' for young learners?

For the purposes of this Young Pathfinder, a 'game' is any fun activity which gives young learners the opportunity to practise the foreign language in a relaxed and enjoyable way. Some activities are simple, both to play and to set up, needing almost no preparation, whilst others are more complicated and require some pre-planning and the use of various materials. Some games have a winner but most are co-operative activities where language practice and fun are the main elements. Dice, counters, boards and cards are not always necessary!

1.   Why use games?

There are a variety of reasons for using games in foreign language sessions with young learners. We can consider them from the perspective of both the learners and the teacher.

As far as **young learners** are concerned,

- for the under elevens play is a natural way of communicating: games appeal to learners' sense of fun;
- games are motivating: the desire to win, or at least to 'have a go' can make even reluctant learners keen to join in;
- young children are energetic and need to participate actively - games link the foreign language to action;
- playing together in this way helps to develop social interaction skills and the ability to work with others, turn taking and sharing.

Many games can be played over and over again and the language items being practised simply changed. This means that learners are familiar with the format and already know what to do, even when the rules are presented in the foreign language. This is particularly the case with games such as 'snap', pelmanism, or dominoes, which are already known to pupils in their own language. With repeated playing, many games become so well known that they can be played independently by pupils in pairs or small groups.

As far as **the teacher** is concerned,

- games are also good fun;
- games take the focus off the teacher;
- games use the foreign language for a purpose and provide a meaningful context for practising new language;
- games provide variety and a change of activity.

For both **pupils and teachers**,

- games contribute to a relaxed, happy atmosphere providing a context within which more effective learning can take place;
- games foster positive feelings about learning another language.

Always prepare your learners thoroughly for games, which should form part of a coherent programme of activities.

2.   Choosing games

Good classroom organisation is necessary, so bear in mind the constraints of your teaching area. Here are some practical points:

*   Is the game going to be an active, noisy one?
*   Is there enough space?
*   What about the furniture? Will you have to move chairs and tables?
*   Who is next door?
*   Would it be better to go into the hall or outdoors?

Next, and most importantly for the busy teacher, you will probably find yourself asking: will I need any equipment or have to produce any extra materials?

Although young learners are often very enthusiastic, it is advisable to allow them plenty of time to become familiar with the sounds of the foreign language without the pressure of having to try to make those sounds themselves. Children can still show you that they are listening with understanding by reacting in some way. It is usually a good idea to select games which practise language recognition (such as those in the 'listen and do' category) before those that require language production ('listen and speak'). So you need to ask yourself

*   Is the game appropriate for my particular class?

In other words, try to think about what foreign language the children will need to understand to play the game, and what language they will need to produce, if any. For instance, if you have been teaching some basic colours, or simple counting, and you want to check that your learners are comfortable with the colours or numbers 1-10, you can proceed as follows.

Get up when you hear...

This is an activity without props and just requires the learners to stand up when they hear either their colour or number called. They do not have to leave their seats.

AIM:	To show understanding of colours/numbers.
MATERIALS:	None.
PRE-TEACHING:	Colours/numbers.

Simply count round the group giving sequences of colours or numbers, e.g. *jaune, bleu, rouge, vert, blanc, noir* or *un, deux, trois, quatre, cinq* (you don't have to start at 1 each time).

You say: *Lève toi, quand tu entends ta couleur/ton numéro!*
Pupils   stand up when they hear their 'cue'.

You can get them all sitting down again by reversing the process.

You say: *Assieds toi, quand tu entends ta couleur/ton numéro!*

VARIATION   *Get up if you're wearing...*

You say: *Lève toi, si tu portes du bleu/du rouge!*
                  (till all the children are up) and then the reverse
                  Assieds toi, si tu portes du vert/du jaune!
                  (till all are down again).

You can see at once if pupils have understood by how they react. Some possibilities for these kinds of listen and do activities form the focus of a later section. As a general rule remember that:

• games need to be short and easily explained;
• games must be simple to carry out.

If the activity you have in mind will take ages to set up, it is probably too complicated!

WHAT ABOUT TEAM GAMES?

At first sight, team games may seem an obvious choice, especially if you are uncertain about setting up pair or group activities and would prefer to work with all the children in your class simultaneously. An example of a simple team game to practise numbers is *Ring the number*.

Ring the number (Entoure le numéro)

AIM: To practise numbers.
MATERIALS: Blackboard and two pieces of different colour chalk.
PRE-TEACHING: Numbers, say 1-10, or 10-20 etc.

You write up each of the numbers once all over the board in white chalk.

You say:	*Entoure le numéro que tu entends!*
Pupils:	As you call out a number, a member of each team runs to the board and tries to be the first to ring the number.
VARIATION	Have two sets of identical numbers, and each team marks its half of the board.

If you wish, you can choose the two team members by name to come and stand at the board or at the front before you call the numbers. This has the advantage of involving less dashing to and fro and is safer! You can also get the pupil who rings the correct number first to choose the next number to call (whisper support if necessary).

And if you are short of chalk, try *Rub out the number/Effacez le numéro* instead. Whichever you choose, remember the height of your smallest child - they must be able to reach the numbers easily!

However, a word of warning: care is needed with team games such as this, in which only one member of each team is involved at a time. We can probably all recall the squabbling that arises over scoring or points being awarded to the opposing side. Furthermore, team games tend to give rise to lots of excitement which itself can degenerate into chaos if not carefully channelled. So,

• try to ensure the maximum participation of everyone.

For instance, here you decide to do the rubbing out yourself or orchestrate a pupil to do so, after a pilot run through. Having covered the board in numbers as before, let the children look at them for a moment.

You say:	*Regardez bien. Maintenant, fermez les yeux!*
	(perhaps even get them to turn away from the board)
	Regardez en arrière/tournez-vous!
	You rub out one or more numbers.
You say:	*Retournez-vous! Ouvrez les yeux! Regardez bien.*
	Qu'est-ce qui manque?Levez la main! Qu'est-ce qui manque?
Pupils	put up hands and call out number(s) missing.

In this version, all children are simultaneously involved in guessing what number has gone, rather than waiting their turn as in the first suggestion.

The kind of comments which we have made about team games are also true of elimination games, where children drop out early on, and afterwards have only limited opportunity to take part. This applies to the old favourite *Simon says*, which is often suggested as a good game to play and yet leaves some players standing at the side almost from the start. Another version of this favourite, which consists simply of giving instructions which everyone tries to carry out, continues to keep everyone involved and is simpler for young learners anyway.

```
 ┌─────────────────────────────────────────────────────────┐
 │ │Helpful phrases│                                         │
 │                                                           │
 │ Debout!                      Steh(t) auf!                 │
 │ Assieds-toi!Asseyez-vous!    Setz dich!Setzt euch!        │
 │ Saute(z)!                    Spring(t)!                    │
 │ Marche(z)!                   Geh(t)!                       │
 │ Cours!/Courez!               Lauf (t)!                     │
 │ Couche-toi!/Couchez-vous!    Leg dich hin!/Legt euch hin! │
 └─────────────────────────────────────────────────────────┘
```

If you do want to play the *Simon says* version, preface some of the instructions with *Jacques a dit* or *Pumpernickel sagt* ..... You can extend these instructions as parts of the body are learned.

A variation is to divide your group into teams and give each pupil a number. When a number is called, all the pupils with that number must carry out whatever instruction you give them. If you wish, you can award points for the first to do so correctly, but often this is not necessary. If you do decide to play games where players are 'out', you can still keep pupils involved for longer by giving children several 'lives' to maintain their interest. Remember, too, that you will need a calming activity to follow a lively game!

WHEN TO PLAY?

Young learners benefit from daily reinforcement of their foreign language skills by means of as many practice activities as possible. Games can be slotted in during any part of the primary day.

If you are the children's usual class teacher, you will be able to decide what point is most appropriate as circumstances dictate. If you are a peripatetic foreign language teacher you will probably find that games can provide a good warm-up activity setting the tone for an enjoyable lesson. They can also end the session on a positive note. To sum up, little and often seems a good maxim.

3. Setting up games

ORAL INSTRUCTIONS

Think about what instructions will be needed in advance. Work out exactly what you want to say in the target language. Do not leave this to chance, since no game will succeed if no one really understands how to play. And if you are uncertain yourself and the setting up takes too long, you are inviting restless behaviour. So,

- keep your instructions short, clear and simple;
- use a limited number of key phrases;
- use words which are similar to English.

Helpful phrases	
Attention!	*Ecoutez maintenant!*
Regardez bien!	*Voici les instructions!*

Don't just read out the instructions - show the children all the equipment they will be using and then demonstrate. This modelling can include the foreign language the children will need to play and is clearer than a lot of talking. Remember to:

- set the task up in small stages;
- explain by showing and doing;
- support what you are saying by gesture and mime;
- use your board or flashcards as support.

You may find it helpful to try out both the game and your 'demonstration' beforehand. In so doing, you may discover that your instructions are still too long or complex. So,

- practise showing how to do something;
- always go for the simplest version!

Build up your own repertoire of instruction phrases in the same way you are doing with your pupils' language - gradually. Don't worry about starting small - concentrate on one or two key phrases which you will always try to use and introduce others step by step.

For example, if pupils are going to play a board game you might like to demonstrate with a pupil. Your demonstration might go something like this:

You say	You do
Attention tout le monde!	Signal you want attention.
Maintenant... regardez!	Ensure they are all watching you.
C'est un jeu de dés.	Hold up some of the equipment.
Voici le plateau de jeux.	Hold up the board.
Voici le dé.	Show the die.
Voici deux pions.	Hold up two counters.
Un volontaire, s'il vous plaît.	Word similar to English.
Merci X, viens ici.	Beckon your volunteer.
X, remue le dé!	Get volunteer to shake die.
Alors, lance le dé!	Volunteer rolls die.
C'est quel numéro?	Prompt your partner.
Trois?	Count aloud.
Tu avances de 3 cases 1 2 3.	Get player to move forward counting.
Maintenant, c'est à moi.	Look pleased.
Je lance le dé.	Roll die with some drama.
Oh la la, je passe un tour.	Miss a turn with mock alarm etc.

WRITTEN INSTRUCTIONS

Generally, you will probably want to rely mainly on oral instructions, since many simple activities appear needlessly complicated if you try to explain them by written instructions.

However, there are occasions when sets of instructions written on card can provide extra support for junior age children playing in small groups, or enable older learners doing a craft activity to start off independently until you have an opportunity to check all is going well. Cooking instructions, enlarged, can be left on display/in the kitchen area for non-teaching assistants, parent helpers or other colleagues to refer to. Foreign language assistants (young native speakers) or parents from the foreign country can often add to a scrapbook of recipes. A bank of such materials will enable other teachers to do the same activity and will provide a record of the spoken language used for the task. So,

• break down the sequence into small steps;
• number each one;
• keep sentences very short;
• support written instructions with pictures.

4. Managing games

BEFORE PLAYING

After you have given the instructions and shown what to do,

- check that everyone has understood and knows what to do.

Don't feel guilty about quickly glossing in English to ensure complete comprehension, but try not to follow up target language with an immediate translation. Your listeners will get lazy if they can anticipate that English will always follow. Try other strategies such as more mime. Say the important bits of your instructions more loudly and slowly, and pause between each step. If this still does not seem to work, perhaps you could use a pupil as an interpreter.

If your pupils have started reading simple captions in the foreign language, use the board or wall charts to display useful questions and answers or phrases. Put up mobiles or inspiration clouds of game playing to help reinforce the language needed.

- Give out the materials.
- Set a time limit.

DURING THE GAME

When you are managing a whole class game,

- let the children take over the caller's role after one or two practice runs with you in charge.

You can always whisper prompts if necessary.

Helpful phrases

Qui veut être le prof?
Des volontaires!

- Use the children as scorers; in a team game you can have two scorers on either side of the blackboard.
- Let the 'loser' in a team game have **one** extra turn next time round.

When the pupils are playing in small groups,

- walk round and monitor what is happening, giving prompts and clarification where necessary;
- as you are observing and listening in to the children you may be able to discreetly make a note of points which perhaps need re-teaching;
- you can also spot individual pupils who are having difficulties.

However, when the aim of the game is communicative, try to refrain from interrupting to correct errors. Whatever type of activity children are involved in, keep up the encouragement and praise. Games are intended to be enjoyable! Here are some praise expressions to help you in this:

excellent ausgezeichnet

génial

chouette *prima*   *très bien sehr gut*

formidable toll $^{10}/_{10}$ *bravo*

super fantastisch   *bon effort!*

TIMING

If pupils are playing card or board games, or constructing something,

- keep an eye on the clock and make sure the activity the children are doing can actually be finished in the time available.

Whether the whole class is playing together in teams, or whether children are playing in small groups or pairs,

- stop whilst everyone is still finding it fun!

5. Teaching ideas

LISTEN AND DO

Understanding spoken language is the first step in learning any foreign language, but as we have suggested earlier, it is also vitally important that the children respond in some way. To begin with, this response will be other than speech. These activities are a particularly valuable way of ensuring that everyone in the class has a chance to take part, and of enabling less able learners to join in on an equal footing with their classmates.

Therefore these first suggestions focus on listen and do activities which can be carried out in a teaching area with fairly restricted space for movement. As colours and numbers are useful right from the beginning, several of the following games can be used to practise counting.

The following games require the learners to show you something, perhaps a flashcard, or an object.

Show me (Montrez moi)

AIM:	To demonstrate understanding of colours by showing a classroom object close at hand.
MATERIALS:	Just what is around in the classroom.
PRE-TEACHING:	Children need to know colours.

You say:	*Montrez moi un objet rouge/bleu/jaune/vert/blanc.*
Pupils	pick up items on tables, in trays: pencils, unifix blocks, whatever is around and matches the colour. This gives pupils a completely open choice.

An alternative is to use either large flashcards or mini flashcards of items connected with the vocabulary area you want to practise.

AIM:	To demonstrate understanding of simple vocabulary by showing a card.
MATERIALS:	Flashcards for colours, numbers, ice cream, food, pets, clothes, etc. If you are using mini flashcards, give out several copies of the same item, as this keeps more children involved at a time.
PRE-TEACHING:	Colours, numbers or whatever the vocabulary is.

You say:	*Montrez moi la couleur jaune!* (for colour cards)
	or simply call out the colours: *jaune! vert!*
	or *Montrez moi le numéro cinq!* (for number cards)
	or simply call out the numbers: *un! sept! dix!*
	or *Montrez moi un T shirt...des chaussures!*
Pupils	wave the appropriate card.

As pupils learn more numbers, include those often confused such as *deux, dix, douze* or *quatre, quatorze* and for older juniors, *quarante; trois, treize; cinq, quinze;* etc. Additional practice can be provided by getting children to hand their mini cards on before playing a further round. This enables you to play several times.

VARIATION	Later you can combine colours and clothes.
	Montrez moi un pull jaune!
	Montrez moi un T shirt rouge!

This kind of language can be incorporated into the daily routine of the class by using expressions such as the following, when pupils are being dismissed for playtime or at the end of the school day.

> *Vous pouvez sortir si vous portez un tricot vert, des chaussettes grises,*
> *une jupe bleue, etc.*

Activities of this kind develop receptive skills, but at the same time offer all pupils the chance to be active participants.

Here are some ideas for games either outdoors, on the field or in the playground, or in the hall where children can walk or run around.

Walking game

AIM:	To practise simple directions and numbers.
MATERIALS:	None.
PRE-TEACHING:	Numbers, and left/right/straight on/forwards/backwards.
You say:	*Cinq pas tout droit, trois pas à gauche!*
	Avance(z) de deux pas, recule(z) de six pas, un pas à droite!
Pupils	carry out actions, walking.

Hiding and finding

Giving directions and instructions can be made more purposeful by hiding articles which learners have to find. Pupils can be involved in the hiding and seeking, giving instructions to the seekers. For these you may need language such as:

Helpful phrases
Va (allez) cacher le/la ....! *Ferme(z) les yeux!* *Ouvre(z) les yeux!*

Helpful phrases
Cherche(z)/trouve(z) ....! *Tourne(z) à gauche!* *Tourne(z) à droite!* *Va (allez) tout droit!* *Arrête(z)!* *Un pas, deux pas!* etc.

And as seekers get closer or not, incorporate expressions such as:

C'est chaud! C'est très chaud! C'est froid!

Running game

AIM:	To show recognition of colours.
MATERIALS:	Any of the following: coloured scarves, bands, small or large beanbags, coloured hoops placed in colour groups around space.
You say:	*Cherchez la couleur: rouge, jaune, vert!* etc.
Pupils	run to beanbag or hoop of appropriate colour.
VARIATION	*Bring me (Apportez moi)*

If you have plenty of beanbags, quoits, coloured scarves or bands, place them around the playing area and give the command *Apportez moi du bleu, du rouge!* etc. This time pupils have to fetch one of the items and bring it to you. If you are anxious about people running into each other in their excitement, you can have several teams, with the items in heaps at the end of the hall, and with only one member of a team going at a time, and everyone running in the same direction.

Dressing up

For this game, children are either in teams in rows, or in groups in a circle. At the end of the hall or in the middle of the circles are bags of clothes. Pupils are numbered off. Call out the numbers of the children, followed by the item of clothing to be put on. It helps if the clothes are somewhat zany - freshly washed clothes from nearly new sales make a good basis for this game.

MATERIALS: Items of clothing duplicated in bags.

You say: *Numéro un! un pantalon!*   *Numéro deux! un pull!*
                  Numéro trois! un chapeau!   *Numéro quatre! des bottes!*
                  Numéro cinq! une écharpe!

Chinese ladders (*Jeu des échelles*)

Another game for teams involves children sitting on the floor, with their legs outstretched to meet the feet of the children opposite. You number the teams, and when the number is called, the children with those numbers must jump up and get to the front of their team by jumping/ hopping, tip-toeing over the legs of the pupils. They then run up the side of their team, over the legs of the pupils at the back, and return to their place.

> ### Helpful phrases
>
> *Asseyez-vous en rang!*   *L'un en face de l'autre!*
> *Pied à pied!*   *Numéro un - marchez doucement!*
> (when they are back)   *Numéro deux - sautez!* etc.

Bonjour / Guten Tag

AIM: To practise greetings.
MATERIALS: None.
PRE-TEACHING: *Bonjour! Salut! / Guten Tag! Tschüss!*

You say: *Mettez-vous en cercle! / Macht einen Kreis!*
                  (get the children into a big circle)
                  You go round the outside tapping each pupil and saying *Bonjour! / Guten Tag!* Unexpectedly insert *Salut! / Tschüss!*
Pupils: Child tapped and greeted with *Salut! / Tschüss!* runs after you. If you reach their place before them, the pupil becomes caller and the game carries on.

The following game is an example of one which can be used with a wide range of topics.

Salade de fruits / Obstsalat

AIM:	To show recognition of a variety of vocabulary.
MATERIALS:	Chairs and space.
PRE-TEACHING:	Present any vocabulary, numbers, fruits, pets etc.

You say:	*Asseyez-vous en cercle!* With children sitting down, you number off the pupils in sequence e.g. *un, deux, trois, quatre, un, deux, trois, quatre* or give pupils different vocabulary items, e.g. *pomme, banane, fraises, orange, pomme, banane.* Make sure there are several children in each of the categories. Pick a category who must swap places. *Tous les 'deux' - changez de place!* *Les oranges - changez de place!*
Pupils	swap places; as they do so, you or the caller also go for an empty chair. Someone will be left without a seat. This pupil left out at the end becomes the caller. At the command *Tout le monde change!* everyone swaps.

You can link the *'all change'* command to almost any vocabulary area: for example, if you are practising colours try *arc en ciel/Regenbogen*, wild animals *zoo/Zoo*, farm animals *ferme/Bauernhof*, buildings in a town *en ville/Stadt*, shops *supermarché/ Supermarkt*, ice cream flavours *glaces/Eis*.

A variation on this game can be set up without needing chairs. Children sit on the floor in circles and are each given a number, colour, animal, day of the week, according to what you are practising. Just make sure that you use each 'label' several times. When the 'label' is called, the children with that label get up and run round their circle. The winner is the person who gets back to their place first. If you have two or three smaller circles, all labelled off similarly, more children can be joining in, but this will depend on the size of your class. One big circle also works, provided you do not use too many categories, and people regularly get a turn to run.

The next game is a variation on musical statues.

Game with music

AIM:	To practise early speaking in the foreign language.
MATERIALS:	Cassette player and cassette of foreign language children's songs.
PRE-TEACHING:	*Bonjour! Au revoir! Ça va? Ça va bien! Comme ci, comme ça!* etc. *Hallo! Tschüss! Wie geht's? Gut! Nicht so gut!* etc.

| You | play the music and stop it randomly. |
| Pupils | move around to the music. When it stops, they shake hands with the person nearest them and say *Bonjour, ça va?* Their partner answers *Bonjour, ça va (bien)* or *comme ci, comme ça, au revoir* or the equivalent in German. |

Le furet

Another running game, played with the children sitting in a circle on the floor, can be combined with the following song, which you can pre-teach. One child has a scarf and walks round the outside of the circle, while the others have eyes closed. The scarf is dropped quietly behind the back of one of the class. At the signal *Qui l'a?* everyone looks behind, and the one with the scarf jumps up and chases the 'furet' who tries to get back to the vacant place in the circle. You can either play the song on cassette, or encourage the children to sing along with the '*Qui l'a? Qui l'a?*' as they play:

Il court, il court, le furet
Le furet des bois mesdames
Il court, il court, le furet
Le furet des bois jolis

Il est passé par ici
Il repassera par là
Qui l'a? Qui l'a?
C'est le chat de Nicolas.

If you feel your learners would respond more quickly to a tune which they already know, you will find an adaptation of *Heads and shoulders, knees and toes* goes down well. Do the actions as you sing, and miss out parts of the body cumulatively after the first run through.

first verse	second verse
tête, épaules	*..., épaules*
genoux, pieds	*genoux, pieds*
genoux, pieds	*genoux, pieds*
les yeux, les oreilles	*les yeux, les oreilles*
la bouche, le nez	*la bouche, le nez*
tête, épaules	*..., épaules*
genoux, pieds	*genoux, pieds*
genoux, pieds.	*genoux, pieds.* and so on!

Playing games in this way gives pupils a feeling of success as they realise just how much they can understand in the foreign language. There are some suggestions for teacher language for organising outdoor or team games in Appendix 1.

LOOK, LISTEN AND MAKE

The foreign language can also be used to make real objects. Seasons of the year such as Christmas and Easter especially lend themselves to art and craft activities. Many children enjoy making something in the paper folding line, following spoken instructions. These activities are usually best done with small groups of pupils at a time, since they can watch each of your movements and at the same time, listen to the instruction that goes with them.

The pages that follow are samples of instructions for making various items, broken down into stages. Please note that these sheets are not primarily intended as reading material for learners, although older children will be able to work from them. Their purpose is to illustrate possible target language which would be spoken by the teacher to accompany each of the actions. You will see that some of the sheets use the singular '*tu/du*' forms, which would be more appropriate if learners were reading the sheets for guidance in making. Others however illustrate the '*vous/ihr*' plural forms for when you are addressing a larger group. In both cases, you might wish to simplify them down still further and it is only expected that learners would absorb key expressions. The original sheets were word-processed in large fonts using Pendown (also available in French) on the Archimedes computer.

Art and craft activities go with almost any topic, and do not always require extensive materials. Suppose, for example, it is Christmas time: you might like to try the thumb print winter scenes of robins in the snow, made with thick squeezy paint: *un rouge-gorge/ein Rotkehlchen* (p18). Or children could make a Christmas card/*une carte de Noël* (p19) or a basket (p19) in which to place small gifts, sweets or, later in the year, tiny Easter eggs. This basket could be made up when the song *un, deux, trois, nous irons au bois* (p29) is being learned. Or during the topic motion, the following making activities can be set up: *un hélicoptère/ein Hubschrauber* (p20); *une toupie/ ein Kreisel* (p21).

For these tasks, children need to become gradually familiar with the words for 'cut', 'fold', 'stick', 'write', 'colour', 'scissors', 'hole', 'circle', 'string', 'triangle'. The necessary language could be taught using flashcards:

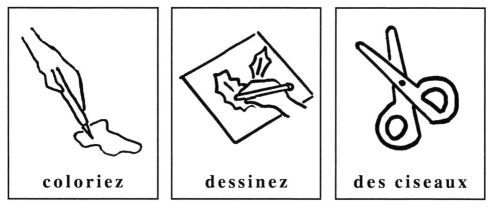

| coloriez | dessinez | des ciseaux |

You write a number next to each flashcard and then call out an instruction, e.g. *coupez!* Learners call out the appropriate number, e.g. *trois!* Reverse this by calling the number and children give you the instruction or item that goes with the number: *deux - les ciseaux! quatre - pliez!* etc. Small cards plus written captions can be used to play card games.

The important thing is that learners are actively using the foreign language in a practical, meaningful way.

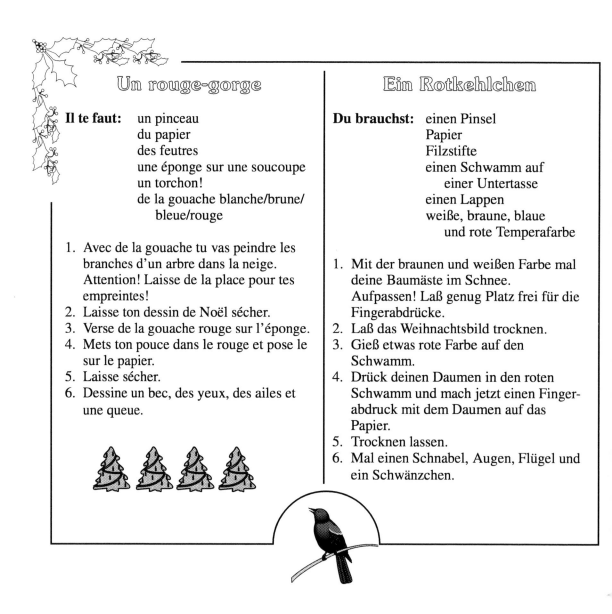

Un rouge-gorge

Il te faut: un pinceau
du papier
des feutres
une éponge sur une soucoupe
un torchon!
de la gouache blanche/brune/
bleue/rouge

1. Avec de la gouache tu vas peindre les branches d'un arbre dans la neige. Attention! Laisse de la place pour tes empreintes!
2. Laisse ton dessin de Noël sécher.
3. Verse de la gouache rouge sur l'éponge.
4. Mets ton pouce dans le rouge et pose le sur le papier.
5. Laisse sécher.
6. Dessine un bec, des yeux, des ailes et une queue.

Ein Rotkehlchen

Du brauchst: einen Pinsel
Papier
Filzstifte
einen Schwamm auf
einer Untertasse
einen Lappen
weiße, braune, blaue
und rote Temperafarbe

1. Mit der braunen und weißen Farbe mal deine Baumäste im Schnee. Aufpassen! Laß genug Platz frei für die Fingerabdrücke.
2. Laß das Weihnachtsbild trocknen.
3. Gieß etwas rote Farbe auf den Schwamm.
4. Drück deinen Daumen in den roten Schwamm und mach jetzt einen Fingerabdruck mit dem Daumen auf das Papier.
5. Trocknen lassen.
6. Mal einen Schnabel, Augen, Flügel und ein Schwänzchen.

Il te faut: une feuille verte
des ciseaux
une feuille rouge
une agrafeuse

1. Plie la feuille verte en deux.
2. Découpe le haut en arrondi.
3. Plie la feuille rouge en deux.
4. Découpe le haut en arrondi.
5. Découpe deux fentes dans chaque feuille.
6. Enfile les bandes vertes dans les bandes rouges.
7. Découpe une bande de papier rouge ou verte.
8. Attache la bande avec l'agrafeuse.
9. Ouvre doucement ton panier.
10. Mets des bonbons ou des oeufs de Pâques dedans!

UNE CARTE DE NOËL

Il te faut: un carton léger
des crayons de couleur

1. Plie la carte en deux.

2. Ouvre la carte et replie vers le centre.

3. Sur les deux volets dessine un sapin de Noël.

4. Ouvre la carte et écris:

5. Copie ce petit poème de Noël:

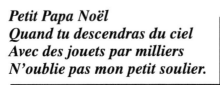

Joyeux Noël
et
Bonne Année

Petit Papa Noël
Quand tu descendras du ciel
Avec des jouets par milliers
N'oublie pas mon petit soulier.

L'HÉLICOPTÈRE   DER HUBSCHRAUBER

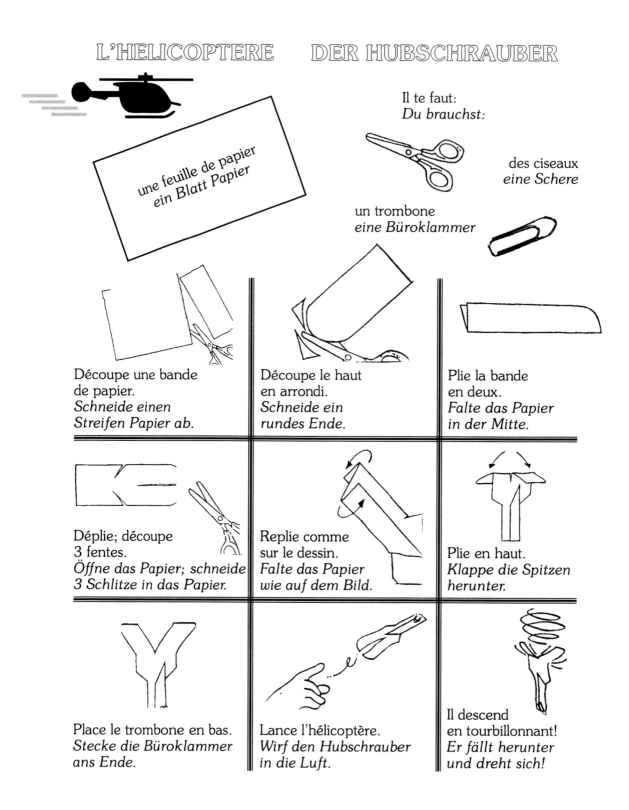

Il te faut:
Du brauchst:

une feuille de papier
ein Blatt Papier

des ciseaux
eine Schere

un trombone
eine Büroklammer

Découpe une bande
de papier.
*Schneide einen
Streifen Papier ab.*

Découpe le haut
en arrondi.
*Schneide ein
rundes Ende.*

Plie la bande
en deux.
*Falte das Papier
in der Mitte.*

Déplie; découpe
3 fentes.
*Öffne das Papier; schneide
3 Schlitze in das Papier.*

Replie comme
sur le dessin.
*Falte das Papier
wie auf dem Bild.*

Plie en haut.
*Klappe die Spitzen
herunter.*

Place le trombone en bas.
*Stecke die Büroklammer
ans Ende.*

Lance l'hélicoptère.
*Wirf den Hubschrauber
in die Luft.*

Il descend
en tourbillonnant!
*Er fällt herunter
und dreht sich!*

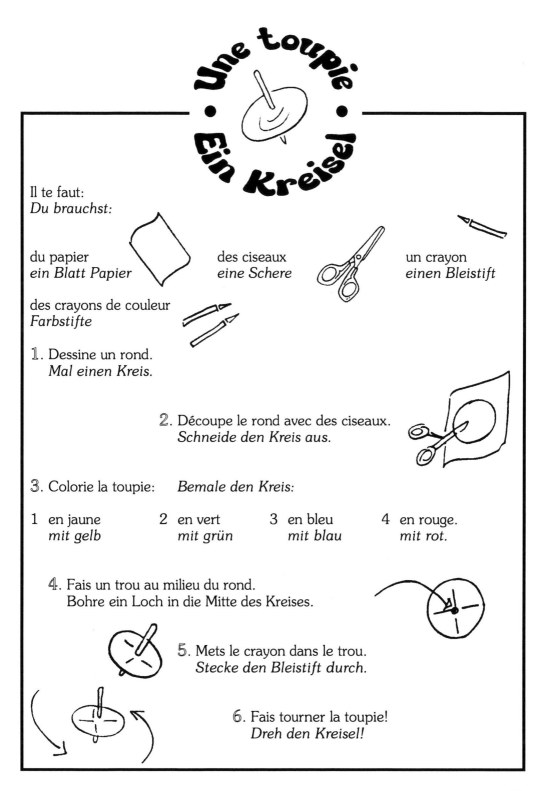

Une toupie • Ein Kreisel •

Il te faut:
Du brauchst:

du papier
ein Blatt Papier

des ciseaux
eine Schere

un crayon
einen Bleistift

des crayons de couleur
Farbstifte

1. Dessine un rond.
   Mal einen Kreis.

2. Découpe le rond avec des ciseaux.
   Schneide den Kreis aus.

3. Colorie la toupie: *Bemale den Kreis:*

1 en jaune
   mit gelb

2 en vert
   mit grün

3 en bleu
   mit blau

4 en rouge.
   mit rot.

4. Fais un trou au milieu du rond.
   Bohre ein Loch in die Mitte des Kreises.

5. Mets le crayon dans le trou.
   Stecke den Bleistift durch.

6. Fais tourner la toupie!
   Dreh den Kreisel!

21

COOKING USING THE FOREIGN LANGUAGE

If you have a kitchen area, small groups of children may be able to make drinks or snacks. The tasting sessions which follow are invariably popular. How about *Caramels au lait*? Omelettes, pancakes and small biscuits are all possible, if you have additional adult help. During a foreign language or European week, some schools have set up foreign language cafés, with children taking the part of waiters and waitresses and serving not only *croissants* purchased from the supermarket, but biscuits or cookies some of them have made following recipes from abroad.

Again, the required language could be taught with the help of flashcards: 'stir', 'pour', 'add', 'grate', 'knife', 'spoon', 'plate', 'pot', 'grater'. This

CARAMELS AU LAIT

1. Allumez le gaz (feu fort).
2. Posez la casserole dessus.
   Mettez-y:
3. 1 tasse de lait.
4. 1 tasse de sucre en poudre.
5. 2 cuillères à soupe de beurre.
6. 2 cuillères à soupe de miel.
   Quand ça bout:
7. Baissez le gaz (feu très doux).
8. Laissez cuire 20 minutes.
   en remuant avec la cuillère de bois.
9. Montez le gaz (feu doux).
10. Laissez cuire 10 minutes.
11. Huilez deux petits moules.
12. Versez-y le caramel.
13. Laissez refroidir.
14. Coupez en carrés.

language for 'making things' can be taught in just the same way as the content language for topics such as pets. Simple drawings can be put on flashcards:

ajoutez **une râpe** **une casserole**

GAMES AT THE BOARD

The next stage is for learners to progress to saying small amounts of foreign language in a stress-free way. The following games all assume that you have a chalkboard or whiteboard to hand and involve some speaking. Some include large or small flashcards. A favourite even with younger children requires a series of mini flashcards, on any topic, blutack and chalk, but otherwise no preparation. It can be set up in a moment.

22

The same or not? (Pareil ou pas pareil?)

AIM:	To practise saying pre-taught vocabulary.
MATERIALS:	Chalk/marker, blutack, up to a dozen flashcards.
PRE-TEACHING:	Words for whatever items are on the cards.

You say:	*Je vais préparer un jeu. Fermez les yeux! Ne regardez pas!*
	Pupils close eyes. You draw 6, 8, 10 or 12 boxes on the board (see below); make sure the symbols you put in each of the boxes each occurs twice. Blutack your flashcards on top in any order.
You say:	*Ouvrez les yeux! Choisissez deux cartes!*
	Pupils call out items on any two cards.
You say:	*J'enlève les cartes! Regardez!*
	You peel the cards off to reveal symbol in box behind.
You ask:	*C'est pareil? Oui ou non?*
Pupils	answer *oui/non.*
	If the cards happen to have covered two matching symbols, those two are removed and the game continues.

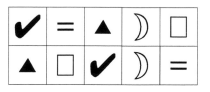

*Cover these symbols
with cards*

This is a memory game which has great appeal and is another form of painless repetition of vocabulary or phrases, such as weather expressions *il pleut, es regnet*, etc. You can start with just three pairs of symbols in six boxes and extend the number to suit the age and ability of the class.

Hangman (Pendu/Galgenspiel)

Juniors who have learned the foreign language alphabet have fun playing very simple spelling games such as *Pendu*, but as children will be concentrating mainly on listening and speaking skills, keep this in reserve and only do this kind of activity with well known words which fit whatever topic you are doing.

AIM:	To practise spelling/saying the foreign language alphabet.
MATERIALS:	Board and chalk/markers.
PRE-TEACHING:	Alphabet and French boys'/girls' names.

You say:	*On va jouer au pendu.*	
	Voilà l'équipe A. |	If you want teams
	Voilà l'équipe B. |	
	Levez la main!	demonstrate
	Devinez une lettre!	

For each letter of the secret word a blank is written on the board. Everyone tries to guess which letters make up the word. You can give support by adding in some starter letters, not necessarily the first one in the word. Pupils can carry on playing with a partner.

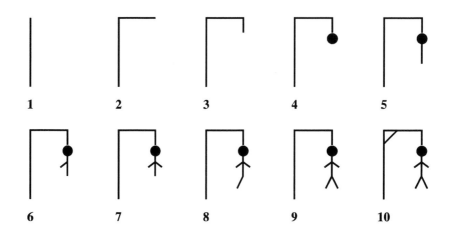

When pupils are learning to talk about their families, the following team game is popular.

How many brothers and sisters do you have? (As-tu des frères ou des soeurs?/Hast du Geschwister?)

AIM:	To practise talking about brothers and sisters incorporating larger numbers.
MATERIALS:	Chalk or board markers.
PRE-TEACHING:	Brother/sister/numbers.

You	draw two sets of boys and girls on the board and put numbers round them as below. Keep your drawings identical!

The children are grouped in two teams. A pupil from each team stands at the board with a marker. Either the teacher or a pupil calls out: *Hast du Geschwister?* And any pupil replies with a 'silly sentence' such as: *Ja, ich habe fünfzehn Schwestern und neun Brüder.* As soon as the sentence is said, the first one at the board to circle the correct number of brothers and sisters wins a point for his/her team. The winner and the loser hand the marker to another member of their team, and the game continues.

Nought and crosses (Morpion/Null und Kreuzespiel)

A popular way of checking understanding and getting learners to produce small chunks of language is to play **Noughts and crosses**. This is one of the games which is already well known and so pupils don't need long explanations. As soon as the grid goes up on the board, they can begin to anticipate what will be happening, so making your task easier.

Imagine children have been learning to ask for ice cream. In this case, you would need to have nine flavours of ice cream, each one represented on a mini flash card. For instance, you could have a card to represent each of the flavours illustrated below:

Draw a grid on the board and blutack each of the cards into a square. Divide your class into two teams, *les croix et les ronds*. Each team calls out the name of an item in turn. Either peel off the mini flashcard and draw in the 0 or X as appropriate, or alternatively have a second blank grid next to your flashcard grid and fill that in as the game goes on. The winning team is the one which completes a line of noughts or crosses.

This game can be adapted to very many topic and vocabulary areas and can also be played effectively on the overhead projector. It can be played with grids of various sizes, you do not have to stick with nine boxes. Grids of 4x4 or 5x5 boxes will allow you to practise getting lines of all sorts of vocabulary.

Choix secret

After you have presented some fresh vocabulary you could play variations on this guessing game.

You say:	*Un volontaire, s'il vous plaît.*
	Viens ici, X.
	To rest of class: *Fermez les yeux! Ne regardez pas!*
Pupil:	makes secret choice of flashcard and hides it behind his or her back.
You say:	*Ouvrez les yeux!*
Pupils	guess the card. *C'est...*

Make this more challenging by calling up a line of up to six volunteers.

MEMORY GAMES

Learners can be encouraged to repeat and practise vocabulary by means of memory games. You can try a simplified version of 'Grandmother went to market and she bought' by keeping to the present tense and saying:

je vais au café et je mange...   *je vais au supermarché et j'achète...*

The next player repeats your sentence and adds on another item. If you think pupils may have difficulty remembering, you can put a flashcard on the board as each item is named, so there is a visual prompt. Alternatively, the beginning letter of the object can be written up, or players be given an envelope in which there are small cards with symbols. The first player takes one and says what it depicts and then hands it on, plus the envelope to the next player.

You can adapt this game by putting all sorts of other items on a list, for instance:

dans ma trousse il y a une gomme, un stylo, un feutre, etc
dans ma chambre il y a ... (furniture)
dans mon armoire il y a ... (clothes/toys)
près de chez moi il y a (town buildings)
à la ferme, il y a (animals)
je vais au zoo et je vois... (animals)

or for older learners, you can vary the tense and introduce:

c'est mon anniversaire, et j'ai reçu ...

Kim's game (*Jeu de Kim/Kimspiel*)

Kim's game can be played with real or pretend objects on a tray or desk top plus a cloth, or with cards blutacked to the blackboard. You can play conventionally.

You say:	*Regardez bien les objets. Qu'est-ce qu'il y a?*
You	name all the items and get everyone repeating them. Then cover the items and ask children to recall as many as possible.
VARIATION	*Qu'est-ce qui manque? Was fehlt?*
You say:	*Fermez les yeux! Augen zu!*
	Remove one or more objects/flashcards.
	Ouvrez les yeux! Qu'est-ce qui manque? Augen auf! Was fehlt?
	Learners guess what has gone.

This game works well with an OHP, and you can take away one or more symbol cutouts instead if you have separate pieces of acetate. If all your symbols are on a single sheet, use post-it stickers to cover up one or more.

If your learners are reading, you can write up the days of the week, or the months of the year, and then rub out one or two whilst children have their eyes closed. Use the same question *Qu'est-ce qui manque?*

SONGS AND RHYMES

These provide an alternative to spoken repetition and are an enjoyable way of developing listening skills in young learners. As most songs are sung by the whole class or by groups within the class, children who are less happy speaking out as individuals can relax and sing along with the rest. The rhythm and music combine to help the words stick in the memory and will often be retained for a long time.

You will find that a number of the children probably already 'know' snatches of traditional French songs such as *Sur le pont d'Avignon.* Not only do these songs have well known tunes, but they are composed around a fairly limited vocal range which suits young voices. Some songs lend themselves to being sung as rounds, for example *Frère Jacques/Bruder Jakob.*

Frère Jacques, frère Jacques,	*Bruder Jakob, Bruder Jakob,*
Dormez-vous, dormez-vous?	*Schläfst du noch, schläfst du noch?*
Sonnez les matines,	*Hörst du nicht die Glocken?*
Sonnez les matines,	*Hörst du nicht die Glocken?*
Ding, dang, dong,	*Ding, dang, dong,*
Ding, dang, dong!	*Ding, dang, dong!*

Even if you are not a brilliant singer, young children are already familiar with finger and action rhymes and enjoy trying out the foreign language versions, especially if they can invent accompanying actions. One favourite is:

Teddybär, Teddybär		*Teddybär, Teddybär*	
Dreh dich um.	(everyone turns around)	*Geh nach Haus.*	(everyone marches on the spot)
Teddybär, Teddybär		*Teddybär, Teddybär*	
Mach dich krumm.	(everyone squats down)	*Mach einen Gruss.*	(everyone bows/waves or shakes hands)
Teddybär, Teddybär			
Spring hinauf.	(everyone jumps up)	*Teddybär, Teddybär* *Zeig deinen Fuss!*	(everyone points a toe)

If you are teaching some parts of the body, the French finger rhyme *Monsieur Pouce* or *Wo ist der Daumen?* in German fit in well. The language is simple with good repetition. Here it is:

Monsieur Pouce est dans sa maison (hide thumb)	*Wo ist der Daumen?* (thumb behind back)
Monsieur Pouce est dans sa maison	*Wo ist der Daumen?*
Toc! Toc! Toc! (tap with fist)	*Hier bin ich! Hier bin ich!*
Qui est là?	(produce hand, thumbs up)
C'est moi! (show one thumb)	*Guten Morgen, Daumen!*
Chut! je dors	(bend thumbs in greeting)
Mais, toc! toc! toc! (tap with other fist)	*Guten Morgen, Daumen!*
Qui est là?	*Weg ist er! Weg ist er!*
C'est moi! Je sors! (show other thumb)	(hands behind back again)

The other fingers can be added in to replace the thumb: *Monsieur Index, Majeur, Annulaire, Auriculaire*; *Wo ist der Zeigefinger/Mittelfinger/Ringfinger/kleine Finger?*

Comptines and counting out playground rhymes are a fun way of helping learners develop a feeling for language. For example:

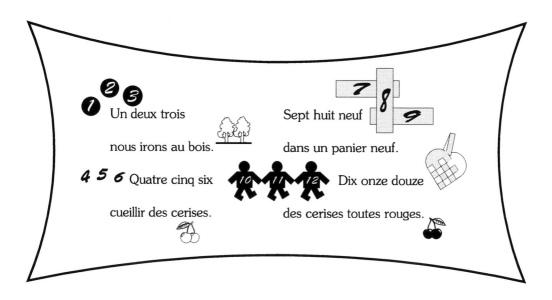

Incidentally, children could also make their own '*panier*' as a craft activity and fill it with little Easter eggs, or sweets for a gift on Mother's Day (see p19).

Then there are the nonsense jingles, along the lines of *Eeny, meeny, miny, mo...*, which have the advantage of usually being short.

Am stram gram	*Eene meene miste*
pic et pic et colegram	*Es rappelt in der Kiste*
bour et bour et ratatam	*Eene meene meck*
am stram gram pic!	*und du bist weg*

Teach songs orally (song sheets in the foreign language are not suitable for young learners). Start by getting children to listen to you singing the song or the cassette. Then pick out a verse and build it up line by line. If there is a chorus or refrain, try starting with that. Don't forget that pictures will support understanding of individual sections. Put actions to the words - the class will come up with ideas! Add your own musical instruments and finally sing along together with increased volume.

6.   Card and dice games

Learners require opportunities to play together not only as a class, but also in table groupings or in a pair. One of the nice things about card, dice and board games is that the element of chance gives all children an opportunity to succeed, and 'losers' can blame their misfortune on bad luck.

CARD GAMES

Lotto (Loto)

Games like lotto help practise receptive skills, with a limited amount of language production at the checking stage. Lotto is often thought of as a game requiring cards and boards, but if you are simply intending to use lotto as a means for practising, say, the numbers 1-10, or 1-20, or letters of the alphabet, the easiest way is to give pupils some rough paper, and ask them to write down a series of letters or numbers within given limits, and to cross these off in pencil as they are called in the foreign language. The winner, who is the first to cross off all their numbers, shouts *loto* or *j'ai gagné/ich habe gewonnen*.

Another way of playing lotto involving little teacher preparation (although as with all games, you must prepare your pupils well before they play) is to get pupils to draw sketches of items on rough paper which they then cross off. This version gives your learners some choice over what to include. If your group is including reading and writing skills, you might like players to write down a few items from a topic you have taught, say four of the days of the week, five months of the year etc and to cross these off.

Alternatively, give out to pupils say three or five small symbol cards each. Call out the cues as before, but this time the pupils turn over any symbol card they have which matches your call so that it is face down on the table. They do this until all their three or five cards are face down. To check that the pupil who has won has turned their cards correctly, the winner must name each of his or her cards as he or she turns them face up again. Of course if you are able to play this with a small group of children, and the children know the symbols and associated vocabulary well, you can gradually increase the number of cards each player has. Even so, about nine is probably the maximum or the game becomes too prolonged.

The game of lotto can give practice in both colours and numbers, if you draw the numbers on the lotto boards in different coloured markers. So for instance, you call out:

> *le numéro onze, bleu*　　　(only players with a blue number eleven may cover it)
> *le numéro trois, jaune*　　(and so on, until the combinations are complete).

Pelmanism *(Jeu de paires)*

All sorts of versions of pelmanism and matching pairs can be played by children in small groups. For younger learners you may like to start with sets of pictures, where two pictures of each item occur in each set. The cards are arranged, face down, either in neat rows on the table top or randomly whichever the players prefer. As in the English version of the game, players turn over two cards at a time, hoping to get a match. It is important that pupils say the foreign language word or phrase for the two pictures chosen, before either claiming them, or putting them back.

> ### Helpful phrases
>
> *Etalez les cartes à l'envers!*   *Vous retournez deux cartes!*
> *Trouvez les paires!*   *Dites le bon mot pour chaque image!*
> *Si les cartes forment une paire,*   *Combien de cartes avez-vous?*
> *vous les gardez!*

When your pupils are matching picture to picture as above, you may find that younger players find it helpful to have one set on a different coloured card from the other. Children then know they have to pick one of each colour. On the other hand, juniors generally like the challenge of having to memorise with no such support, and two sets on the same colour card can be suitable for them.

If you are playing games with juniors which involve, say, pictures and words in the foreign language which have to be picked up and matched, it is a good idea to have the symbols or pictures on cards of one colour background, and the words on cards of a different colour background. Older learners may like to match foreign language word to English word.

The same principles of combining symbols and symbols, or pictures and words, or word to word also apply to versions of dominoes. If you are going to make dominoes or sets of cards with pictures of objects to practise vocabulary such as fruits or food, you can cut out pictures and stick them on the card. Cut out the objects or symbols away from any distracting background.

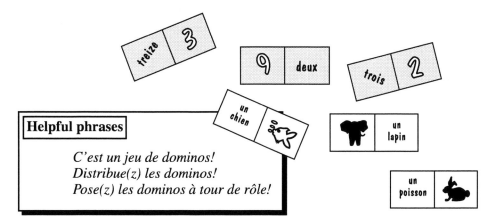

> ### Helpful phrases
>
> *C'est un jeu de dominos!*
> *Distribue(z) les dominos!*
> *Pose(z) les dominos à tour de rôle!*

Snap (Bataille)

You need sets of cards, with each theme represented four times. Players take it in turns to place a card down. As they turn it over and place it on the pile they must say what it is in the foreign language. If they put a matching card down to the one on the top of the pile, they can claim the pile, provided they named the card correctly as they laid it down. The winner is the player who gets all the cards. For instance, if learners have been pre-taught pets:

Pupil A puts down a hamster   *un hamster*
Pupil B puts down a cat   *un chat*
Pupil A puts down a cat   *un chat! bataille!*

Players could count the number of cards they have at the end in the foreign language.

Happy families (Le jeu des familles)

This is a versatile game which can be adapted to suit almost any area of vocabulary. For each group of players, you will need sets of small pictures all mounted on card of the same size. There should be several clearly distinguishable 'families', e.g. classroom objects, clothes, food etc with four items per 'family'.

You say:	You do:
Il faut collectionner des familles complètes.	Use word similar to English.
Battez les cartes comme ça!	Shuffle the cards.
Donnez ... cartes à chaque personne!	(depending on the group sizes and number of cards) Give some cards to a volunteer.
Il y a quatre cartes par famille.	
Si vous avez cette carte-ci,	Hold up a card.
vous dites à un autre joueur 'Tu as...?'	Turn to your partner.
Si votre partenaire a...	
il dit 'Oui, voilà/oui, j'ai...!	
Il vous donne la carte.	Get your partner to pass you the card
Si votre partenaire n'a pas la carte,	Shake head
il dit 'non, désolé'.	
C'est le tour du prochain joueur.	

The other 'members of the family' to be collected can be indicated on the cards thus:

Dominos en chaîne

For children who have been learning the foreign language for some time, here is a simple domino style game which combines listening, speaking and reading! For this, prepare cards in sequence as follows:

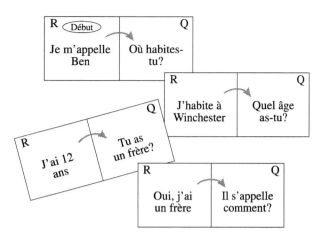

Mark the starter domino *Début*. Hand out to pupils. It does not matter that everyone does not get a card! Say: *On commence par ce domino-ci* and show a larger card with the word *Début*. Then start the sequence off with the trigger question: *Bonjour, comment tu t'appelles?* The pupil with the domino with the statement which matches the question, here perhaps *Je m'appelle Ben*, must listen and reply. They then ask the question which is on their domino, for example: *Quel âge as-tu?* and so the sequence is built up. This kind of practice can be made quite short for beginners, or extended as children learn more structures and vocabulary items. Dominoes can be handed on and the activity repeated with different players.

USING DICE

Young learners enjoy rolling really large soft dice of the kind supplied for babies, and counting the number of dots. You may be fortunate enough to come across some of these second hand in nearly new or bring and buy sales.

To extend counting practice, dice with various numbers of faces beyond six can be purchased, and of course more than one die can be rolled at a time. As they roll the dice, pupils say aloud the numbers, and ask each other *C'est quel chiffre?* and keep a running tally of the scores.

> **Helpful phrases**
>
> *J'ai un six et un trois.*
> *J'ai un double six.*
> *Ça fait combien?*

You can practise simple arithmetic by incorporating plus and minus signs on the dice faces (blank jumbo 50x50 mm dice can be bought for you to customise).

Why not let some children make their own dice? They can either colour in each face, and move forward to the appropriate colour on a board (rather than counting forward squares) or they can put their own dots on.

As a variation on cube dice, pupils can make their own spinners (see p21); these can be divided into different numbers of sections, and adapted for colours, numbers or symbols to cue a variety of language practice.

Younger children can practise colours by playing **Rainbow towers/Tour de perles**. Similarly, you can always use the colours or numbers on the dice to encourage children, to construct towers with unifix cubes, adding the colour and number according to the combinations thrown.

FABRIQUE UN DÉ

BASTLE EINEN WÜRFEL

Il te faut: de la colle
Du brauchst: *Klebstoff*

des crayons
de couleur
Farbstifte

des ciseaux
eine Schere

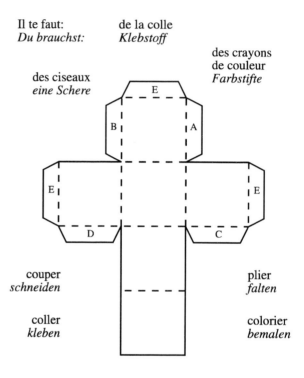

couper   plier
schneiden   *falten*

coller   colorier
kleben   *bemalen*

Beetle games

For younger learners dice games in which each number on the dice allows a certain feature to be added to a basic shape are more suitable. These games are variations on 'beetle' which children will already be familiar with. As children roll the dice they need to say the number in the foreign language and also name the object they are going to add to their basic shape.

Helpful phrases
Jouez en groupes de quatre!
Il faut commencer par 'un six' pour (le corps).
Si tu lances un 'un', tu as...
Si tu lances un 'deux', tu as...

The house that Jack built (*Bâtir la maison*)

Players throw a coloured die and build parts of a house: windows, doors, garage, roof, chimney etc. Start with white to get the house shape. An instruction card might say:

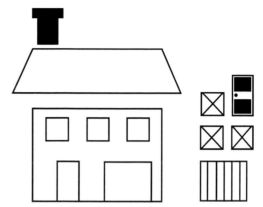

le vert - une fenêtre
le jaune - une porte
le bleu - un battant de porte du garage
le rouge - un toit
le noir - une cheminée (si tu as un toit;
sinon tu passes)
le blanc - tu passes

Primary learners also enjoy using travel versions of 'Guess who?' to identify various faces by asking and answering questions on hair, glasses, eyes.

Pupil game language

If you want everyone to join in, you need to teach some of the phrases required to keep a game going, so that players do not become stuck in the middle. This will be especially the case when children are going to continue playing in pairs or small groups, and for the dice, board and card games we have mentioned. But introduce game playing language in extremely small doses, and aim to build up key expressions over a considerable period of playing time. Be realistic. You could choose the expressions you feel are most important from the list in Appendix 2.

7. Making your own materials

If your school is unable to fund the immediate purchase of a foreign language course for young learners, you can still make some materials of your own which you will be able to re-use again and again.

FLASHCARDS

You will need A4 sheets of coloured card to serve as large flashcards. These can be cut in half to provide you with two A5 flashcards. Smaller cards (approximately 12x15cms) are also available through school suppliers and are the smallest size suitable for whole class work.

You will also need some thick marker pens in various colours to draw bold outlines. (You will find that smaller width fibre tip pens do not show up very clearly and will only be suitable for illustrating small game cards.) Bold colours which contrast well are more easily seen from the back of the classroom than subtle pastel shades. Too much blue and green together tend to merge if they are too close together.

The role of visuals is to support the learning and practice of new language, which means that learners must be able to see at once what your visuals represent. So,

• make your drawings or choose drawings which are as clear and unambiguous as possible.

A good source of ideas for quick sketches of the 'matchstick person' type can be found in Andrew Wrights's *1000 pictures for teachers to copy*.

Coloured pictures, cutouts from gift wrap and advertisements from foreign language magazines are a rich source of flashcard objects. Calendars in particular provide beautiful animal pictures and can be purchased very cheaply around the end of January!

You may find it helpful to write in pencil on the reverse side of your flashcard what it represents. You can also put a dot in the top right hand corner on the back so you can hold it up away from you and be sure that it is up the right way!

CARDS FOR GAMES

Lots of games such as versions of lotto or matching pairs, use small cards. These can be made by making a master on white A4 paper of the visuals you want. By folding a sheet of A4 in half once lengthways, and then in half widthways, and in half once again, you will have 8 playing card size rectangles. Stick your visual into each of these eight boxes and then photocopy onto coloured A4 card. Two hints:

- if you want your 'playing cards' to be used for adaptations of card games such as *Snap, Happy families* etc then make sure you stick your visual on the card upright

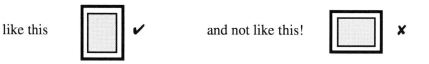

like this   ✔   and not like this!   ✗

You can use the type on the right for dominoes or pelmanism type games, but not for traditional card games, where the players are dealing out the cards and placing them on piles. If you use the type on the left for all your card games, you have a more versatile set. Alternatively, you may wish to work with square cards, rather than rectangles.

- it is generally not advisable to make a coloured card master and photocopy directly from this. The coloured background often photocopies black and the image is no longer very visible.

Cards that belong in the same pack should be the same colour so that they can be collected easily at the end of sessions. Put an identification mark on the back, so you know which set or game they belong to.

To save time, ready made blank white playing cards, originally provided through Waddingtons, are available for purchase from the address in the resource list. These will save you ruling out master sheets and cutting out. Mini cards (3.5x4.5 cms) in a variety of colours, suitable for matching pairs or lotto items can also be purchased.

You can quickly make attractive cards to practise counting and letters of the alphabet by mounting various coloured 'peel off' stickers for pre-schoolers onto these white playing cards. You will find sheets of these stickers in many toy and bookshops.

Lotto boards

If you have time to make lotto bases, you can use large card divided into sections with symbols for the board. Some squares can be blanked out, and boards with as few as four squares are suitable for beginners. As you call out each item, pupils use small pieces of scrap paper to cover the items which match your call. You need to keep a list as you go. In all versions, you can check if you have a genuine winner by asking the winner to read back their answers.

BOARD GAMES

First a word about the construction of board games. Commercially sold board games tend to be based on a square board, but home made adaptations on an A4 rectangle shape can be preferable. This is mainly to facilitate the making of masters, which can be prepared on white paper for photocopying. These dimensions make storage of the 'boards' a smoother process, since you will find that you need to store your playing surfaces as flat as possible. If they are A4, you can slide them into plastic wallets and keep sets in ringbinders. This has the advantage of preventing the edges getting turned up. If boards are stored without this extra protection, the uneven surface means that the counters tend to slide around and not remain in place during games.

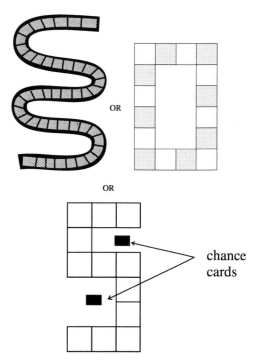

You can make a board with a track of interconnected squares: a grid of 5x5 squares will give you 25 squares, which is about right. Otherwise board games can go on too long. However, young learners sometimes become confused about the direction of play when they are moving their counters. So a more obvious shape is required as in the examples on the right.

In order to make board games more challenging, you can write instructions for the players to follow as they make their way around the board. These can either be written on the board itself, e.g. when a player lands on a square s/he may find the question *C'est quoi?* and have to name what is in the square, or have to give the French for a colour or object: *C'est de quelle couleur?* or *Qu'est-ce que tu dis?*, *C'est quel animal?* etc. These kind of questions give rise to language production on the part of the learners as they move along the track. If you wish, you can add instructions such as *Avance de 3 cases! Passe un tour! Recule de 2 cases!* as your pupils get accustomed to playing. And of course players count aloud as they move around.

However, writing the instructions straight onto the master copy does have the disadvantage of the whole master copy needing to be redone, or at least your mistake tippexed out if you happen to make a slip as you are writing, especially as the squares are likely to be fairly small. Another possibility is to write instructions onto a set of 'chance' cards which can be placed near at hand and from which players can select one

at certain points in the game. By adding to or taking away from your instruction cards, you can make your game tie in with the stage of your learners and with the topic which you are practising. These games of course require some reading and are more suitable for junior age children.

ACETATES FOR THE OHP

Several of the games suggested can be undertaken with the support of the overhead projector, which enables you to be very versatile with presentation and repetition. You can use silhouettes or even stencils of shapes effectively for guessing games by revealing bit by bit of the whole. If you are going to photocopy directly from materials such as *Idées pratiques pour la classe de français* (MGP, 1991), then do make sure you are using the heavy duty photocopiable acetate. The thinner variety, for writing on only, will melt in the machine. And of course you can add a whole variety of colours to overlays and cutouts, or indeed draw the originals yourself. Again simplicity is paramount.

A final point about visuals, whether on flash cards, small cards, or acetate,

• always be consistent.

Use the same symbols/pictures on your small cards as you do on your large flashcards.

STORING MATERIALS

To ensure that cards and boards have as long a life as possible, it is helpful if you can laminate them - a straightforward process which you may be able to carry out at your local Teachers' Centre or in a technical support unit if you are near a teacher education establishment. However, this is not essential. If you are making games for pairwork, it is important that player A does not see at the beginning what Player B has, so use separate envelopes for A and B. Sometimes you might need a screen between players (an atlas usually works).

Cards or acetate symbols can be stored in small envelopes, with the flap folded over and held in place by a paper clip. Old shoe boxes are suitable for storing envelopes or pieces for games; otherwise a variety of plastic storage wallets are available, or even freezer bags. Remember to label everything clearly for speedy access!

Conclusion

Finally, I should like to acknowledge the inspiration drawn from all the children whom I have observed playing foreign language games. My thanks are due too to the foreign language assistants and class teachers who have allowed me into their classes, to the native speakers who have made suggestions for target language, and to primary teachers who have shared ideas for activities.

We all believe that games and game-like activities are a central feature of a good language teacher's repertoire. They are not an optional extra, but an essential part of the learning process, especially in the teaching of younger children. Research indicates that games are at least as effective as alternative instructional techniques. Most importantly, they help enhance learners' self esteem and can promote positive attitudes towards language learning, particularly when they are appropriately integrated with other strategies. There are a huge number of other games which lend themselves to learning a foreign language, and we hope that this Young Pathfinder will inspire you to go on collecting, and perhaps creating your own games.

Appendix 1 Teacher language

SETTING UP GAMES

attention	attention please	Ruhe! pass(t) auf bitte
bon, écoute(z) (maintenant)	listen	hör(t) gut zu
regarde(z) bien	look at the board	schau(t) auf die Tafel
regarde(z) par ici	look this way	sieh (seht) hierher
voici les instructions	here are the instructions	hier sind die Spielregeln
voici une démonstration	here's an example	hier ist ein Beispiel
lève-toi (levez-vous)	get up	steh(t) auf
assieds-toi (asseyez-vous)	sit down	setz dich (setzt euch)
jouons	let's play	wir wollen spielen
un volontaire/des volontaires svp	a volunteer/volunteers	Freiwillige bitte
viens (venez) ici	come here please	komm(t) hierher bitte
montre(z)-moi	show me	zeig(t) mir
touche(z)	touch	fass(t) an
écris/écrivez	write	schreib(t)
dessine(z)	draw	zeichne(t)
répète/répétez	repeat	wiederhole/wiederholt
dis/dites à ton/ta/ votre partenaire...	ask your partner...	frag(t) deinen/euren Partner/ deine/eure Partnerin
tu comprends?/vous comprenez?	do you understand?	verstehst du?/versteht ihr?
comment dit-on... en anglais?	how do you say... in English?	wie sagt man... auf Englisch?
c'est quoi en anglais?		
que veut dire...?	what does... mean?	wie heißt das...?
qu'est-ce qui manque?	what's missing?	was fehlt?
jouez en groupes de deux/ trois/quatre	play in groups of two/ three/four	spielt zu zweit/dritt/viert
joue(z) avec un(e) partenaire	play with a partner	spiel(t) mit einem (einer) Partner(in)
à tour de rôle	in turns	der Reihe nach/wechselt euch ab
à vous maintenant	over to you	ihr seid jetzt dran

INDOOR GAMES

le dé/les dés	die/dice	der (die) Würfel
une toupie	spinner	der (die) Kreisel
le pion/les pions	counter(s)	die Spielmarke
le plateau de jeux	board	das Spielbrett
la case	a 'square' in a board game	das Feld
place(z) ton/votre pion sur une case	put your counter on a square	leg(t) deinen/euren Spielstein auf ein Feld
le départ	start	der Anfang

l'arrivée	finish	das Ziel
lance(z) le(s) dé(s)	throw the die/dice	roll(t) den/die Würfel
avance(z) de deux cases	go forward two squares	zwei Felder nach vorne
recule(z) de trois cases	go back three squares	drei Felder zurück
relance(z) le(s) dé(s)	have another throw	roll(t) den/die Würfel
passe(z) un tour	miss a turn	einmal aussetzen
le gagnant/la gagnante	the winner	er/sie hat gewonnen
mélange(z) les cartes comme ça	mix the cards like this	misch(t) die Karten so
distribue(z) les cartes	deal the cards	teil(t) die Karten aus
étale(z) les cartes à l'envers	spread out the cards face down	leg(t) die Karten mit dem Gesicht nach unten hin
retourne(z) deux cartes	turn over two cards	dreh(t) zwei Karten um
prends/prenez une carte	pick up a card	nimm (nehmt) eine Karte
collectionne(z) les paires	collect pairs	sammel(t) Paare
collectionne(z) une série de...	collect a set of...	sammel(t) eine Reihe von...
dis/dites le bon mot	say the right word	sag(t) das richtige Wort
combien de cartes as-tu/ avez-vous?	how many cards do you have?	wieviele Karten hast du? (habt ihr)?
pose(z) une carte	put down a card	leg(t) eine Karte hin

OUTDOOR GAMES

asseyez-vous/mettez-vous en cercle	sit in/get into a circle	setzt/stellt euch in Kreisform
asseyez-vous (?)/mettez-vous en rang	sit in/get into a line	setzt/stellt euch hintereinander hin/auf
les uns derrière les autres	one behind the other	einer hinter dem anderen
face à face	opposite each other	einander gegenüber
dos à dos	back to back	Rücken an Rücken
une équipe	a team	eine Mannschaft
l'équipe A commence	team A starts	Mannschaft A beginnt
au signal	at the signal	beim Zeichen
à tour de rôle	in turns	der Reihe nach
un pas à droite/gauche	one step to the right/left	einen Schritt nach rechts/links
deux pas en avant	two steps forwards	zwei Schritte vorwärts
trois pas en arrière	three steps backwards	drei Schritte rückwärts
change(z)	change	alle wechseln
défense de courir	don't run	nicht laufen
à vos marques	on your marks	Achtung
3-2-1 partez	3-2-1 go	eins zwei drei los

Appendix 2 Pupil language

PUPIL TO TEACHER

excusez-moi	excuse me please	Entschuldigung
vous pouvez m'aider?	can you help me please?	können Sie mir bitte helfen?
je ne comprends pas	I don't understand	ich verstehe nicht
vous pouvez répéter?	can you say it again?	wiederholen Sie bitte
qu'est-ce que je dois faire?	what do I have to do?	was soll ich machen?
comment dit-on... en français?	how do you say... in French/ German?	wie sagt man... auf Deutsch?
je ne sais pas	I don't know	ich weiß nicht
je n'ai pas de partenaire/crayon	I don't have a partner/pencil	ich habe keinen Partner/Bleistift
une feuille de papier, s'il vous plaît	can I have a piece of paper?	etwas Papier, bitte
J'ai fini	I've finished	fertig

PUPIL TO PUPIL

qui commence?	who's going to start?	wer beginnt?
je suis A	I'm person A	ich bin A
tu es B	you're person B	du bist B
tu es mon/ma partenaire	you're my partner	du bist mein(e) Partner(in)
tu es mon adversaire	you're my opponent	du bist mein(e) Gegner(in)
c'est à qui?	whose turn is it?	wer ist dran?
c'est à moi/toi; c'est mon/ton tour	it's my/your turn	ich bin/du bist dran
attends	wait a minute	Moment bitte
tu triches	you're cheating	du mogelst
répète	say that again	wiederhole/noch einmal bitte
vas-y	come on	fang an/mach schon
continue	carry on	weitermachen/weiterspielen
donne moi...	give me...	gib mir...
c'est à moi/toi	that's mine/yours	das is mein/dein
j'ai gagné	I've won	(ich habe) gewonnen
non, ça ne va pas/c'est faux	that's wrong	das geht/stimmt nicht
désolé(e)	sorry	tut mir leid
passe un tour	miss a turn	aussetzen
reste là	stop there	bleib da
tu as fini	you've finished	du bist fertig
arrête, tu as gagné/perdu	stop, you've won/lost	stopp, du hast gewonnen/ verloren

Useful sources

Resources for French

Bruzzone C, *French just for kids* (Berlitz, 1992)
Handbook + 3 cassettes

Garabedian M and others, *Les petits lascars* (Didier for CREDIF, 1987-88)

Idées pratiques pour la classe de français (Mary Glasgow Publications, 1991)

Kay J, *Un kilo de chansons* (Mary Glasgow Publications, 1978)
Cassette of 12 songs, lyrics and teacher's notes

Le Hellaye C and D Barzotti, *Farandole* (Hatier/Didier, 1992)
Pupil's book, workbook, teacher's book, 2 cassettes

Meyer-Dreux S, *Le petit trampoline* (CLE International, 1994)
Pupil's book, teacher's book, 2 cassettes

Meyer-Dreux S and others, *Trampoline* (CLE International, 1991-)

Muffin (series) (Muffin Canada, 1986-1989)
Cassettes + songbooks. Series includes *'Comment ça va?'*, which contains Rock 'n' Roll version of *Frère Jacques*

Nyburg A, *French for fun* (Harrap, 1991)
Book and cassette

Nyburg A, *Further French for fun* (Harrap, 1991)
Book and cassette

Resources for German

Bruzzone C, *German just for kids* (Berlitz, 1992)
Handbook + 3 cassettes

Nyburg A, *German for fun* (Chambers Harrap, 1991)
Book + cassette

Praktische Ideen für den Deutschunterricht (Mary Glasgow Publications, 1992)

Seeger H and T Vieth, *Wer? Wie? Was?* (Gilde Buchhandlung Carl Kayser, 1989-)
2 cassettes, glove puppet, 5 readers (see also Wahl M, *Lieder machen Spaß*)

Wahl M, *Lieder machen Spaß* (Gilde Buchhandlung Carl Kayser, 1993)
Songbook + cassette which supports *Wer? Wie? Was?* (see above)

Non language specific resources

Artfile-creatures (Graphic Books International Ltd, PO Box 349, Newlands Building, Lowlands, Guernsey, 1990)

Christmas (Graphic Books International, 1991)

Generalisable game activities in modern language learning (Language Learning Journal no. 8, September 1993)

Guess who? (MB Travel Pax) for 2 players

Rainbow Towers (Spears Games) for 2-4 players

The house that Jack built (Spears Games) for 2-4 players

1000 pictures for teachers to copy by Andrew Wright (Collins)

Other resources

Plain white playing cards, small cards in multi colours and jumbo white dice - available from Technical Support Unit, University of Reading, Bulmershe Court, RG6 1HY.
Tel: 01734 318690

Templates and stencils for pre-schoolers - available from Early Learning Centre/Woolworths

Unusual shaped dice and ready made playing cards - available from Miniflashcard Language Games, PO Box 1526, London W7 1ND